D1263093

A Day in the Life: Rain Forest Animals

Jaguar

Anita Ganeri

Heinemann Library
Chicago, IL

www.heinemannraintree.com
Visit our website to find out
more information about
Heinemann-Raintree books.

To order:
☎ Phone 888-454-2279
💻 Visit www.heinemannraintree.com
to browse our catalog and order online.

Edited by Nancy Dickmann, Rebecca Rissman, and
Catherine Veitch
Designed by Steve Mead
Picture research by Mica Brancic
Originated by Capstone Global Library
Printed in the United States of America in Stevens Point,
Wisconsin.

062011
006232RP

**Library of Congress Cataloging-in-
Publication Data**
Ganeri, Anita, 1961-
   Jaguar / Anita Ganeri.
      p. cm.—(A day in the life. Rain forest animals)
   Includes bibliographical references and index.
   ISBN 978-1-4329-4106-2 (hc)—ISBN 978-1-4329-4117-8
(pb) 1. Jaguar—Juvenile literature. I. Title.
   QL737.C23G3612 2011
   599.75'5—dc22
                                        2010000962

Acknowledgments
We would like to thank the following for permission to
reproduce photographs: Ardea pp. 4, 17, 23 cub, 23 mammal
(Nick Gordon), 13, 23 jaws (Thomas Marent); Corbis
pp. 6 (Flame/© DLILLC), 7, 11, 19 (© Frans Lanting),
12 (Encyclopedia/© W. Perry Conway), 14, 23 prey
(Encyclopedia/© O. Alamany & E. Vicens), 20 (© Kevin
Schafer), 22 (© Tom Brakefield); FLPA p. 18 (Minden Pictures/
Gerry Ellis); Getty Images p. 10 (National Geographic/Steve
Winter); Photolibrary pp. 5 (Oxford Scientific (OSF)/Elliott
Neep), 9, 23 swamp (Index Stock Imagery/Mark Newman),
15 (Oxford Scientific (OSF)/Carol Farneti Foster), 16
(age fotostock/Peter Lilja), 21 (Animals Animals/Lynn Stone);
Shutterstock pp. 23 rain forest (© Szefei), 23 skull
(© Gualberto Becerra).

Cover photograph of a jaguar reproduced with permission of
Shutterstock (worldswildlifewonders).

Back cover photographs of (left) a jaguar's jaws reproduced
with permission of Ardea (Thomas Marent); and (right) prey
reproduced with permission of Photolibrary (Oxford Scientific
(OSF)/Carol Farneti Foster).

We would like to thank Michael Bright for his invaluable help
in the preparation of this book.

Contents

Some words are in bold, **like this**. You can find them in the glossary on page 23.

What Is a Jaguar?

A jaguar is a **mammal**.

Many mammals have hairy bodies and feed their babies milk.

tiger

Jaguars belong to a group of mammals called big cats.

Tigers are another type of big cat.

What Do Jaguars Look Like?

Jaguars have strong bodies with short, thick tails.

They have a large head, strong **jaws,** and sharp teeth.

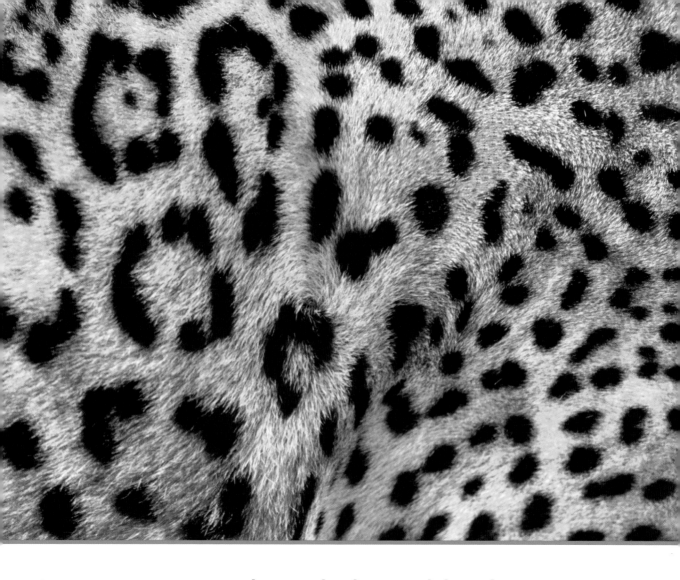

Most jaguars have light, golden-brown fur covered with black spots.

Some jaguars have very dark fur and look almost black.

Where Do Jaguars Live?

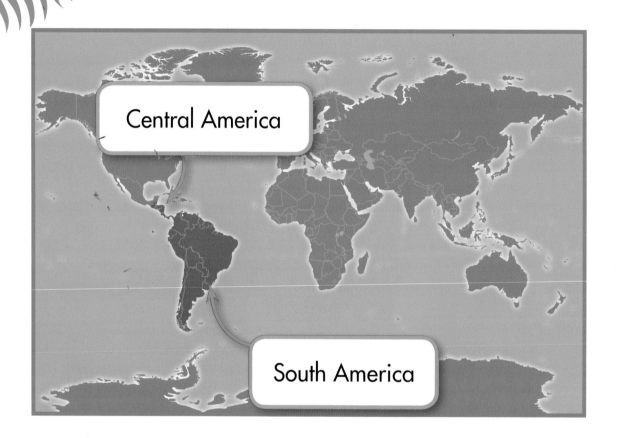

Central America

South America

Jaguars live in the **rain forests** of Central America and South America.

It is warm and wet in the rain forest all year long.

Jaguars live near rivers and **swamps**.

They hunt for food in the water and on land.

What Do Jaguars Do at Night?

In the evening, jaguars start hunting.

A jaguar may hunt all night long.

Jaguars have special eyes that can see in dim light.

This helps jaguars to find their **prey** at night.

How Do Jaguars Catch their Food?

At night, jaguars hunt for **prey** in the rain forest.

A jaguar hides among the trees and then suddenly pounces.

jaws

A jaguar has strong **jaws** and sharp teeth for catching its prey.

It can kill an animal by biting right through its **skull**.

What Do Jaguars Eat?

deer

Jaguars hunt many kinds of **rain forest** animals.

Some of these are large animals, such as deer and wild pigs.

turtle

Jaguars also catch **prey** in the water, such as fish, frogs, and turtles.

Their teeth are sharp enough to bite through a turtle's shell.

Do Jaguars Live in Groups?

Jaguars live on their own.

Each jaguar roars loudly to keep other jaguars away from its patch of forest.

cub

Jaguars only meet up when they are ready to have **cubs**.

Jaguar cubs live with their mother for up to two years, learning how to hunt.

What Do Jaguars Do in the Morning?

In the morning, a jaguar goes out hunting.

Many **rain forest** animals are just waking up, so there is plenty of **prey** around.

Sometimes, a jaguar stops by the water's edge.

It waits for an animal to come get a drink, then it leaps on its prey from behind.

What Do Jaguars Do During the Day?

After hunting, a jaguar spends most of the day resting or sleeping.

A jaguar sleeps for about 12 hours a day.

Sometimes jaguars rest in caves by the riverbank.

Sometimes they climb **rain forest** trees and go to sleep on the branches.

Jaguar Body Map

fur

ear

tail

eye

leg

paw

whiskers

Glossary

 **cub** baby jaguar

 **jaws** top and bottom parts of the mouth

 **mammal** animal that feeds its babies milk. Most mammals have hair or fur.

 **prey** animal that is hunted by other animals for food

 **rain forest** thick forest with very tall trees and a lot of rain

 **skull** bony part of the head that contains the brain

 **swamp** wet, muddy land

Find Out More

Books

Huntrods, David. *Jaguars*. New York, NY: Weigl
   Publishers, 2007.
Walker, Sally M. *Jaguars*. Minneapolis: Lerner
   Publications, 2009.

Websites

www.bigcatrescue.org/cats/wild/jaguar.htm
www.arkive.org/jaguar/panthera-onca/
www.sandiegozoo.org/kids/animal_profile_jaguar

Index